T0208969

GOD*versations:*
Crafting **YOUR** prayer life

Roscheeta M Brundige

WESTBOW
PRESS®
A DIVISION OF THOMAS NELSON
& ZONDERVAN

WestBow Press books may be ordered through booksellers or by contacting:

WestBow Press
A Division of Thomas Nelson & Zondervan
1663 Liberty Drive
Bloomington, IN 47403
www.westbowpress.com
844-714-3454

Scripture taken from the King James Version of the Bible.

ISBN: 978-1-6642-3491-8 (sc)
ISBN: 978-1-6642-3492-5 (hc)
ISBN: 978-1-6642-3490-1 (e)

Library of Congress Control Number: 2021909993

Print information available on the last page.

WestBow Press rev. date: 12/06/2021

This book is dedicated to the following:

To the best God-momma ever, Linda Rosa Bennett. She taught me how to push, persevere, praise, worship, teach, and be thankful. Her smile and unconditional love lit up my life. I will never forget her being a mother, aunt, friend, and confidante. She was the voice of reason and always encouraged me to live, not just exist. I miss you much, Sunshine.

To Mother Carrie Cleone Applewhite. She remembered the Word of God verbatim and could quote whole chapters. She would sit on the altar to pray and call out all the names of the membership of our church and their families, as well as the names of her children, grandchildren, and extended families. She even remembered the names of the visitors. She always told me to do what was right. She would say, "If you try, you will." I dedicate this to her strength and fortitude.

To Mother Ellen Jones, a.k.a. my spiritual grandmother. If this woman did not take my parents under her wing when they were new converts, my life would have been totally different. I appreciate her love, wisdom, and power. One of the last times I saw her, she said, "If you learn the Word and work it like you do those puzzles, you will be baaaddd!" Well, Mother, I'm on my way to being baaaddd!

To Big Momma, Alice Jones. She was a praying woman. She loved God and family, and she taught us to love one another. She helped build several churches in Buffalo, New York. She survived the South and moved north, but she never lost her love for people.

To my momma, Helen Louise Brundige. I love this woman. In some ways, we are just alike, and in others, we are opposites. She is the woman who gathered her children together for devotion before school. She is the one who taught us consistency with God. Even during illness, trials, and tribulations, she continued to love her children and other people's children. I am grateful to be her child and to have her face (inside joke).

To my daddy, Joseph Brundige. I love this man. He has always believed in me and supported me. He has been the greatest financial backer of all my business and life endeavors.

ACKNOWLEDGMENTS

I thank my heavenly Father, Jesus, and the Holy Spirit for salvation and leading me in all truth and making all things possible.

Thank you to my family. I appreciate all your understanding and support.

Thank you, Pastor Johnny H. Kidd, and First Lady Ruby Kidd. Your teaching and love gave me the love for God's Word, which made this book possible.

Thanks to Evangelist Ella Gill. I appreciate your introduction to Mother Dabney. Your weekly teaching on prayer and your dedication to the prayer line encouraged me and kept me inspired in this endeavor.

Thanks to the radio baby, Adel Anthony, for believing in me before I even started.

Thank you to my book coach, Tialie Simpson, for keeping me in line to get it done.

Last but not least, thanks to the best best friend ever, LaRonda Monique. You know.

CONTENTS

Introduction xi

Chapter 1   My Prayer Story 1

Chapter 2   What Is Prayer? 4

Chapter 3   Why Pray? 10

Chapter 4   How to Pray 18

Chapter 5   When and Where to Pray 23

Chapter 6   Types of Prayer 25

Chapter 7   Why Is Prayer Your Responsibility? 29

Chapter 8   How to Start 31

Chapter 9   Final Thoughts 34

Chapter 10   Prayer Prompts and Journaling Pages 35

My Favorite Resources 105

INTRODUCTION

I was brought up in a spiritual environment, where teaching was the focus of our spiritual journey. We were taught to be independent. We were expected to apply those teachings and to independently learn the Word, learn to love God, and learn to hear from God. We were never expected to wait for the middleman to get us to God. We were taught to be individual thinkers and believers. We were taught that it was all right to disagree, but it didn't mean we had to be disagreeable. We were taught to look beyond the name and denomination on the door of a church and see the heart of the believer, comparing all that we saw with the Word of God. During my teenage years, and on through my thirties, I didn't realize what I really had and how it would form my life naturally and spiritually.

I still apply what I've learned in every area of my life. Even in my teaching, my intent is to encourage others to be independent and take their spiritual growth in their own hands by laying a foundation in prayer and the Word of God. This way, we will not be led astray by false doctrines, false prophets, manipulators, or abusers.

Prayer is near and dear to my heart for several reasons, which we will explore in this book. I want to encourage you to relax and read this with an open heart and mind. I also want you to feel God's love for you and His call to you through these pages.

As you read, I want you to gain confidence in prayer. I want that confidence to create a desire to talk to God. I want you to be intentional about your spiritual development. I want you to gain insight into the heart of the Father.

1

My Prayer Story

How it all began:

When we were children, my mother gathered my sister, my brother, and me around her for devotion before school (Dad worked during the day). Someone would sing. Someone would pray. Someone would read a scripture. And someone would testify. None of those things were new to us since we were brought up in church. We grew up in a praying household. Were we perfect? Definitely not. But we prayed through it all.

I vividly remember my first answered prayer. My sister left to live with my aunt and uncle in New York for a while. We had never been separated. We were like Frick and Frack. I couldn't imagine my life with her gone. I was heartbroken and devastated. I couldn't believe she left me. I felt so abandoned, hurt, and disappointed. I was empty. I don't remember how old I was, but I do remember lying in my bed, all covered in pink (my favorite childhood color), and crying so hard that my body convulsed; the only thing I could say was, "Oh, God." I couldn't speak any sentences or form coherent thoughts. I couldn't quote any scripture. There was no song to usher in the presence of the Lord. All I had were my sincerity and my brokenness, and that was all God needed. Then as the tears subsided and my breathing normalized, I felt the most amazing thing: God wrapped His arms around me and comforted me. It was the most remarkable feeling ever. The warm cocoon of His love enveloped me. He helped me. I slept, and I knew I would be all right.

I was an adult when this memory came back to me. It came forward with so much clarity. I know beyond a shadow of a doubt that God is real. Not only is He real, but God hears, and He answers prayer. He is concerned about His children. We are never left alone. We don't have to find the right words, right phrase, or the right praise and worship song. We don't have to do acrobatics or flips and jump through hoops. We just need to turn to God and lay it all out before Him, verbally or not. You don't even need words to pray. God knows your every thought and every issue in your heart. Our job is just to give it to Him, to freely abandon all boundaries and cast it all on Him. Give it to Him. He can carry it. He can handle it. He knows exactly how to fix it. He has full knowledge and the experience to handle every problem and situation. He is a sovereign God, a holy God, and a righteous God. He will not turn a deaf ear.

Lay your head on His shoulder and cry, scream, holler. Throw a temper tantrum, even. God is there to pick up all the broken pieces of your heart, life, and soul. He doesn't care if it's in shambles or not.

He binds up the wounds and heals the brokenhearted. God will give you joy for sorrow and beauty for ashes. It's the greatest exchange policy ever. *Ever.* He will always give you the long end of the stick. (Who wants the short end?) He is the wonderful Counselor. He is the Prince of Peace. He can bring you to a place of peace, where there is no chaos or confusion.

So you would think with that experience, I would never fall away or turn away from God. Well, I was insecure in my teen years, thinking I was less than. I was less than smart, pretty, talented, and so on. I gave my life to the Lord as a teenager, but it seemed too hard, so I made a vow. I told the

Lord that I would be saved after graduating high school, and one year after graduation, just before my nineteenth birthday, I gave my life to the Lord.

I was on fire. I was praying, reading my Word, and encouraging myself through song and music. I was fasting, praying, and writing. Gradually, with the challenges of life, finishing college, dating, church work, and family, the fire dwindled down. There were points of rekindling, but without my participation in maintenance, it would repeatedly die out.

Fast-forward to my midthirties. I was thoroughly dissatisfied with my life in general. After chasing external things, I changed my focus to inward things. I began to consistently pray for God to show me myself. Well, He did, and I was not happy. I was angry for about a year. Yes, a year. I was angry because when you grow up in church, you think you know how to do this saved thing. I realized that what I knew was all hearsay. I was lacking a personal relationship with the Lord and lacking in knowing His Word.

So that is where my journey began. I joined prayer groups and started actually doing daily devotionals, not just collecting them. At times when I didn't know what to do or where to go, there would be a testimony or sermon about daily prayer, Bible study, worship, or personal time with the Lord. I realized that God did not want perfection, but He wanted a purposeful relationship. He wanted me to desire to spend time with Him. He wanted me to want Him just because of who He is and not for what He can do.

A lot of what is included in this book is from what I learned from observation, personal experience, trial and error, and direct downloads from the Lord.

What Is Prayer?

Prayer Is Two-Way Communication

Prayer is two-way communication between you and God. In the body of believers, we seem to focus on several different forms of one-way communication. Prophecy, visions, and the preached Word come from God to us. Worship and praise are from us to God. So prayer is you communicating to God and God communicating to you. It's a conversation. It is give-and-take.

Who Is Involved in Prayer?

You and God are involved in your prayers—as well as Jesus and the Holy Spirit.

God has already communicated with you through His Word. Yet He desires to hear from you as well. Prayer is your call for clarity and revelation of what God is speaking in His Word.

God is our Father. He created us in His image. He provides, protects, teaches, forgives, and loves us, just like our natural fathers.

Ephesian 4:6 says, "One God and Father of all, who is above all, and through all, and in you all."

Psalm 68:5 says, "A father of the fatherless, and a judge of the widows, is God in his holy habitation."

Isaiah 64:8 says, "But now, O Lord, thou art our father; we are the clay, and thou our potter; and we all are the work of thy hand."

Jesus is our intercessor. He is the risen King and Word made flesh.

Romans 8:34 says, "Who is he that condemneth? It is Christ that died, yea rather, that is risen again, who is even at the right hand of God, who also maketh intercession for us."

The Holy Spirit is our comforter, teacher, speaker of truth, and even our memory.

John 14:16 says, "And I will pray the Father, and he shall give you another Comforter, that he may abide with you for ever."

John 14:26 says, "But the Comforter, which is the Holy Ghost, whom the Father will send in my name, he shall teach you all things, and bring all things to your remembrance, whatsoever I have said unto you."

John 15:26 says, "But when the Comforter is come, whom I will send unto you from the Father, even the Spirit of truth, which proceedeth from the Father, he shall testify of me."

For example, I say, "Holy Spirit, I invite You into my heart, mind, and body today. Take over my life. Be with me throughout the day. Abide in my house and car and on the job. Cover me, and overshadow me. Let the cloud of Your glory rest and dwell with me. Guide me like the children of

Israel. Be a cloud by day and a pillar of fire by night. Lead me in a plain path, and show me the way I should go."

Yes, you should invite Him. You can send an invitation. You should be a gracious host, if you will allow me to use that term, just the way you invite your guests over for dinner. You greet them, you make them feel welcome, and you serve them. You meet whatever needs they have, spend time with them, and give them your attention. You listen to them and make them comfortable. Yes, invite Him in. It'll make all the difference in your prayer life.

It will make a difference in you. Who are you in Christ? Are you an unbeliever who never received Jesus as your Savior? Are you a backslider? Are you newly converted? Have you been saved for some time? Do you know what the Word of God says about you?

Who Are We Praying To?

As believers of Jesus Christ, we pray to God. God is the Creator of the heavens and earth. He created humanity in His image.

Let me introduce you to the Alpha and Omega, the beginning and the end. He knows your end. He knows which way to take you so you have good success. God can help you come out unscathed and whole, just like the three Hebrew boys came out of the furnace without any sign of being in the fire. No soot or burns. They didn't even smell like fire, smoke, or any such thing. That is the type of God you have. He desires to work on your behalf. He wants a relationship with you. He wants to spend time with you. He wants to get to know you. Yes, *you.*

God is not an attention-seeker. He isn't doing acrobatics while waiting for you to pay attention to Him. He is a Father, standing quietly in the wings, waiting for you to realize how good He is. He wants to solve your problems. He wants to answer your prayers. He wants to hear your side of the story. He is waiting for you to be vulnerable with Him.

We are often vulnerable with people in our lives: family, friends, teachers, church leaders, coworkers, therapists, and the list goes on. But we can always be vulnerable with God. He never shares our secrets or puts us on blast. He comforts us even when He is chastising us. He is there for us, saying, "Daughter [son], come to me. I can fix it."

You don't have to handle it alone. You don't have to keep going around the mountain. You don't have to keep going around in circles, over and over again. There is no issue too big or too small for God. There is nothing too silly or trivial to share with Him. There is no such thing as wasted prayer. God wants you to share it all; He wants to give you all, and it all starts in prayer.

Sometimes, what we need is revealed to us through someone we know. We all have a circle of people, and each person in that circle has a circle of people. God often uses this network to answer prayer, to teach us, to motivate us, and to help us. For instance, your son's teacher is married to an engineer who works for a company that needs your services. After meeting this teacher, you are eventually awarded the contract, which elevates your business in ways you've been praying to God to manifest.

Well, I'm going to be that person for you today. My goal is to introduce you to the one Person Who will make all the difference in every situation in your life. This is the Person Who's most concerned about you, Who thinks you are the best thing since sliced bread. This is the Person Who made sacrifices and moved heaven and earth, just for you. He has provided every need since the beginning of time.

In case you haven't figured it out, I'm talking about God, Abba Father, the Alpha and Omega. I'm talking about the true and living God. He is the God of Abraham, Isaac, and Jacob. He is the God Who parted the Red Sea. He is the God Who rained fire from heaven. He is the God Who saved the three Hebrew boys from the fiery furnace. He is the same God Who kept Daniel in the lion's den. He is the God Who led the children of Israel with a cloud by day and a pillar of fire by night. He is the same God Who sent His Son Jesus to die on a cross as a sacrifice for your sin, to redeem you to Him. He is the God of all creation. He made everything with you (yes, *you*) in mind.

Perhaps you're thinking you don't need an introduction. However, sometimes you need a new perspective on a familiar concept.

We often need to change our view of God. It is important that we lose our self in God through fervent prayer and supplication. We must totally trust God with all of life's issues and cast every care on Him because He cares for us. Yes, even in our sin, He cares for us.

Before we were created in our mother's womb, God cared for us. He wants to spend time with us. Even in Genesis, God walked in the garden with Adam. Not as a manager, overseer, or boss, but as a Father, friend, and confidante. God loved Adam. He created Him, formed him in His image and likeness, and breathed the breath of life into him. Isn't that love? It's this same love that parents have for their unborn child, unseen yet loved. Parents love their children even when they are wayward, hard-headed, obstinate, disobedient, or rebellious. The parent will still love the child. You will still do whatever you can for them, give whatever you can to them. If you, being human and imperfect, are willing to give your child good things, even when they mess up, how much more does the heavenly Father, being perfect, righteous, just, and faithful, want to do for you?

I want to say, "Hi [insert your name here], meet God the Father. God the Father, meet [insert your name here]."

Now have a seat. Take some time, and get to know each other. Get to know God's characteristics. God is so big, you will never know the whole of Him, but I promise you, the more you learn, the more you will want to learn, and it all begins with prayer.

Let me reintroduce you to the One Who will heal you. Did you know that He is the great physician? He is the God Who heals you. Did you know that He is the wonderful counselor? He won't spread your secrets or give out your medical records. You don't need HIPAA when you deal with the Father. He is the Prince of Peace. During chaos, He can give you peace.

You don't have to buy it or earn it; just receive it. He is your shelter. He will protect you from further harm. He is a God you can trust. I mean, you've tried everything else. Just give Him a good old college try. Know that He is a fierce God, and He will fight for you. He will fight for what is right. He will fight for your needs. He will be your protector. You can take the walls down that you have built around your heart because you're safe with God. You can be vulnerable with Him, and He will not use it against you.

Now let me introduce you to Jesus Christ, the righteous one. He is the Word (God's Word) in flesh. He was sent by God to be a Savior for all. He was born of a virgin and lived to become an adult and perform miracles, signs, and wonders. He died a sinner's death so we can be redeemed to the Father.

Now let me introduce you to the Holy Spirit. Some refer to Him as the Holy Ghost. The Holy Spirit is power. In the beginning, God spoke the Word (Jesus) and created the earth. The power of the Holy Spirit moved upon the earth and completed the work of the Word. He is a teacher. He is discernment. The Spirit also teaches us to pray.

> Likewise the Spirit also helpeth our infirmities: for we know not what we should pray for as we ought: but the Spirit itself maketh intercession for us with groanings which cannot be uttered. (Romans 8:26)

> And he that searcheth the hearts knoweth what is the mind of the Spirit, because he maketh intercession for the saints according to the will of God. (Romans 8:27)

3

Why Pray?

Jesus Prayed

Even Jesus prayed often, persistently, and fervently. He always consulted with the Father through prayer, so we should follow His example. We don't have to do everything on our own. We don't have to be perfect or have all the answers. God has all the answers. He is the answer. The ever-present, all-knowing, and all-powerful God is working on your behalf.

Motivation to Pray

Motivation: How to obtain it? How to keep it? How to fuel it?

Motivation is what a lot of us lack in many areas. We don't have a big enough "why." Why do you want to build a prayer life? Why did you pick up this book? Why are you in pain or discomfort? Mine was a major dissatisfaction. I was tired of being in a dry place. I was tired of depending on others to experience the presence of God and waiting to hear from Him.

Prayer is work, and it requires discipline. We find it hard to be consistent, timely, faithful, dependable, and steadfast in the things we pursue. Prayer is like any other task that takes discipline. It takes discipline to develop a personal prayer life and set aside time to spend with the Lord consistently. It takes discipline to overcome sleepiness, tiredness, busyness.

Sometimes, we feel like we are not in the right mindset, headspace, or heart space to pray. Sometimes, we feel like we don't know the right words to say. Sometimes, we can just come into His presence and sit and whisper that we need Him, and He will come in and fellowship with us. Prayer is not about the right phrase, the right question, or the best delivery. I've found that picturing God sitting next to me in my prayer space makes it easier. You wouldn't keep your bestie waiting, would you? Would you keep the doctor waiting for you to show up to your appointment? Would you let your children wait for hours and days to be picked up from school or practice? Definitely not, but we make God wait to talk to us. We make Him wait to spend time with us. Why do we hurt Him so? Is it because He is a great, big God, and He is so full of love that He isn't disappointed when we break our date with Him?

How to Obtain Motivation

Why do you need to pray? Why did you pick up this book? What pain do you have that needs to be addressed through prayer? What is your "why"? Where do you see yourself going, and how do you see your life changing? Your answers to these questions are your reasons to be motivated. This is what you will refer to when times get hard and when you don't feel like praying or being dedicated.

How to Keep Motivated

To keep your motivation, you will need to submerge yourself with testimonies of answered prayers and transformation of lifestyles. You may have memories of previously answered prayers when you take time to remember those it builds motivation. Reading and hearing the testimonies of answered prayers from others helps build motivation as well. One book that motivates me to keep my prayer life on track is *What It Means to Pray Through*, by Mother

Elizabeth Juanita Dabney. This book lit a fire in my prayer life. Hearing stories of miracles, signs, and wonders propelled me to seek God more. You can even find testimonies of answered prayer in scripture. Hannah prayed for a son, Elijah prayed for rain, David prayed for deliverance, and Jesus prayed for God's will to be done. Search out some prayers in the Word that speak to you and your situation. Study them, knowing that God answered them and that He hears you and will answer you.

How to Fuel Your Motivation

First, pray often. Consistency will build your desire to pray. Second, ask God for a mentor or prayer partner. You may need to join a prayer group or team. Lastly, get to know other people who pray. They will inspire and encourage you if you want to fall off.

Why Is Prayer Important?

Prayer is the most effective way to experience the richness of God's love.

Are we not aware that He wants and desires to spend time with us? He created us for that purpose. Yet we put everything before Him, while claiming to love Him. We honor everyone else above Him, but we say we are in a relationship with Him.

Prayer is the best way to have a great relationship with the Lord. If you aren't spending time with and communicating with the one you love, you are in a bootlegged relationship. For your relationship with the Father to work, you need to have communication, and that is done through conversation: prayer. Talking *with* Him, not to Him. After speaking, listen and take heed to what you hear. You should take note and study what He likes. You should do what He likes. It's a relationship, a healthy relationship.

Some of us are looking for a great relationship, someone to love us fully and completely. However, we turn away from the One Who loves us unconditionally. God will never leave you or forsake you. He is always concerned with you. He is concerned with every aspect of your life, from the most minor problem to the most major issue. He wants to meet with you. He wants to answer your questions. He wants to show you His ways. He wants to show you a way around your obstacles and mountains.

God is right there, waiting. Why are you making Him wait? Why are you avoiding Him? Why are you avoiding His voice? Why are you refusing to be intimate with Him? Why are you choosing to have a raggedy relationship, when He wants to have a balanced relationship with you?

Who turns down a healthy relationship that is full of unconditional love? God has moved heaven and earth to bring you to this point, and you still want to break His heart? You still want to cause Him pain? You still reject Him? Can you imagine the hurt, pain, and sorrow that He endures each time you break a date with Him? Whether it's your personal or corporate prayer, Bible study, or worship time, God is always there, waiting for you. He is wanting you, desiring you and only you. You are welcome to bring your problems and issues. He has taken the limits off. There are no boundaries. You can freely abandon yourself to Him, and He will not harm you. He has great expectations for you. He is just waiting for you to come to Him. God is waiting.

He wants to hear what is on your heart and mind. He wants to know the things that keep you up at night, nag your brain all day, and hurt you. He also wants to hear your secrets, the things you don't talk about because of hurt, pain, disappointment, anger, frustration, bitterness, and hatred. These are things you are afraid will overwhelm you and cause you to lose control. These are the things He wants you to give to Him. He can handle it. It won't scare Him away, like it did your last significant other. He won't leave you like your so-called friends did. He will be there to help you through it all. He will bear the burden if you let Him. He will ease your pain, wash you clean, and wipe away your past. He will allow all the things that you went through to catapult you into a place where He is glorified, and you are justified. He can create your testimony from the very thing that brought you shame. Who can do that but God? Who can heal you but God? You've tried other things: sex, drugs, eating, bullying, promiscuity, changing your gender and sexual partners and persuasions, and still you are empty, lonely, and hurting. So why not let God have it?

You've been carrying it for a long time, a very long time. You have been weighed down for so long, going through the motions of being happy and wearing a mask that says you are OK, all while dying inside.

Benefits of Prayer

Why pray? A better question is, why not? Prayer is the best therapy and form of communication. It allows you to vent, cry, plead, and pour out your heart to the only Person Who has the power to change situations, places, things, and other people. Who can know the deceitful heart of man? No one but God. He is able to change your perspective, habits, dreams, thoughts, and purpose. God sees the end of every situation before it even begins. Prayer can lift sadness and depression.

Why prayer? Because prayer is the best form of communication. God has already written a love letter to you that is the best sixty-six books of love, instruction, comfort, guidance, assurance, and faith. Now He wants to reveal the truths of it to you. God has already communicated to us through His Word. Prayer is your call for clarity and revelation of what God is speaking in His Word.

The effectual fervent prayer of the righteous avails much. Not righteous as in perfect but righteous as being made right with God through Jesus Christ. We can ask anything in His name, according to His will, and He will give it to us. Prayer is a natural stress-reliever. It will lighten your burden and help put things into perspective.

Prayer: The Best Therapy

There are several different forms of therapy. The one thing about prayer is that you can pray anywhere. You don't have to wait for your therapist appointment or for a psychoanalyst to fit you in. We have direct access to the Father and all His resources. Unlike other therapists, we are not limited to their finite knowledge. We have the all-knowing God to counsel us. Earthly counselors need to figure us out before they can offer an avenue of help or assistance. God does not have to get to know us because He knew us before we were in our mother's womb.

Before I formed thee in the belly I knew thee; and before thou camest forth out of the womb I sanctified thee, and I ordained thee a prophet unto the nations. (Jeremiah 1:5)

For he knoweth our frame; he remembereth that we are dust. (Psalm 103:14)

Solutions and Resources

Did you know that prayer is the least-sought-after solution? It always seems to be our last resort instead of our first resource. We try everything in our power to change a situation and work things out, but then when we find it's too big for us (and sometimes not even then), we turn it over to the Lord. We just keep beating our head against the wall, waiting for it to become a door. Why do that when you know the One Who can make a door? We will go around and around the same situation before we give it over to God. We just learn to adapt and dwell in the place of discomfort or trouble, instead of giving it over to the problem-solver. Sometimes, we don't give things to God because we don't think we deserve it. Sometimes, we don't think He will do it. We know He can but don't believe He will.

Sometimes, we are afraid of the route the Lord will take us to change a situation or fix the problem. Will it cause us even more pain or harm or discomfort? Will it bring about too great of a change? Will I have to move out of my place of comfort? Will I have to change my habits? My friends? My life? My lifestyle? Let me help you: If you must change any of that, the Lord will help you. He will strengthen and comfort you. He will show you how to go on in a life of newness, change, and difference. God is a good Father Who gives good gifts, so if the route to your deliverance is difficult, you can trust that God will provide a way. He will turn things around in your favor.

There hath no temptation taken you but such as is common to man: but God is faithful, who will not suffer you to be tempted above that ye are able; but will with the temptation also make a way to escape, that ye may be able to bear it. (1 Corinthians 10:13)

And we know that all things work together for good to them that love God, to them who are the called according to his purpose. (Romans 8:28)

Sometimes, we can't see what is in our favor because it's not the way we would have planned it. God's plan has an end already established; it's just a matter of getting you there. When we fix it, we know how we want it to end, but there are no guarantees that it will be that way. Why not go with the experienced one, God the Father? He knows all, sees all, and controls all. He is sovereign, so we should trust Him, and the beautiful thing is that we have an open door to Him. He doesn't hide Himself from His children. He said to ask, seek, and knock so it will be given, found, and opened. Plain and simple. He wants to help you. He is the answer.

Pray to the Father. He is the answer to every question and the solution to every problem. Jesus is the answer, point-blank. Jesus is the answer, period. Jesus is the answer, end of story. Jesus is the answer; the book is closed.

Results of Prayer

Prayer can be used for every facet of life, for any reason. You can pray about anything: love, strength, trouble, hurt, pain, disappointment, joy, laughter, job, sex, marriage, singleness, children, money, home, debt, and the list goes on and on. There are scriptures that address any area you want to pray about.

Prayer Improves Your Spiritual and Natural Life

Prayer improves your life, naturally and spiritually. Prayer helps you to relax. Prayer helps soothe symptoms of illness and improves health. I've talked with others who have the habit of praying, who said that prayer lowers blood pressure and soothes headaches. Prayer can heal your body. Prayer gives you peace. Prayer improves confidence. Prayer gives you courage. Prayer provides you with a solution and answers your problems. Prayer will help you have clarity in thought. Prayer will help you live authentically. God will show you who you really are, and you can live your life being you (authentic).

Prayer helps you get closer to God because you become more familiar and more intimate with Him. Prayer will cause you to have a revelation of God's Word. Prayer will give you clarity in spiritual things. Prayer will improve your discernment. Prayer will push you to be delivered. Prayer not only increases the desire to be spiritually whole, but in prayer, the game plan is given to you, bit by bit. Prayer brings about the spirit of repentance. Prayer will heal your spirit.

Prayer Lets You Feel the Warmth of His Love

The Holy Spirit comforts us when we come to the Father in prayer. As we cry on His shoulder and put all our concerns before Him, not only is there the lifting of burdens but there's comfort in His embrace. There is comfort in knowing that even before circumstances change, we can have peace that God is going to take care of us. We find His love waiting to console us. His love is there when we don't deserve it, when we haven't earned it, and when we have gotten ourselves into trouble. He doesn't withhold love from us.

We need to learn how to receive the unconditional love of God. As humans, we only know conditional love. We are used to people withdrawing love from us when we don't behave like they want us to. We often project the actions of others onto the Lord and expect Him to respond in the same way. God loves us with an everlasting love. He doesn't take it back. He keeps his Word. He is faithful to us.

Listening Ear

We are able to take everything to the Lord. Not just spiritual things but also all things that pertain to your life (2 Peter 1:3). The Lord is not judgmental when we pray. He always listens and responds with the correct response, every time. God keeps our secrets. He doesn't throw our faults back in our face. He doesn't gossip about us behind our backs. He is patient and attentive with us.

4

How to Pray

Study prayer. Don't be afraid to take an academic approach to studying prayer and the Word of God. In my studies, I've found that once I decide to study, God will direct me. I started off with a concordance, a dictionary, and a notebook. I look up words and reference scriptures about the text that I'm studying. I pray and wait in expectation to receive understanding and revelation. You'll be amazed at what the scriptures will reveal to you. Even when studying something you've read before, God will give you revelation knowledge and the tools to apply it to your life. Pray according to God's will. In the garden of Gethsemane, Jesus prayed twice about going to the cross, but He quickly prayed, "not my will but Your will." If we are going to see a move of God in our lives and experience miracles, signs, and wonders, we must submit to God's will. In order to know His will, we must study His Word.

> And he went a little farther, and fell on his face, and
> prayed, saying, O my Father, if it be possible, let this cup

pass from me: nevertheless not as I will, but as thou wilt. (Matthew 26:39)

He went away again the second time, and prayed, saying, O my Father, if this cup may not pass away from me, except I drink it, thy will be done. (Matthew 26:42)

And this is the confidence that we have in him, that, if we ask anything according to his will, he heareth us: And if we know that he hear us, whatsoever we ask, we know that we have the petitions that we desired of him. (1 John 5:14–15)

Model Prayer

I love to use the Lord's Prayer as a model prayer. There are many other examples in the Bible, including the prayer of Jabez (1 Chronicles 4:10), Jesus praying at Gethsemane (Matthew 26:39), and Jesus praying for the disciples (Luke 17:6–26, Luke 22:31–32). For this book, we are going to focus on the Lord's Prayer. Jesus taught the disciples these words when they asked Him how to pray.

After this manner therefore pray ye: Our Father which art in heaven, Hallowed be thy name. Thy kingdom come, Thy will be done in earth, as it is in heaven. Give us this day our daily bread. And forgive us our debts, as we forgive our debtors. And lead us not into temptation, but deliver us from evil: For thine is the kingdom, and the power, and the glory, for ever. Amen. (Matthew 6:9–13)

This prayer consists of greeting the Lord, honoring Him, and submitting to His will. It recognizes God's provision, asks for forgiveness, and seeks to forgive, while also asking for guidance and deliverance, followed by honoring God's power.

Building Your Prayer

There are some basic things to understand when praying according to the above model prayer. We are to include these things in our prayer:

- Honor. We honor God by referring to Him our Father.
- Thanksgiving. We should be thankful to God.
- Repentance. We repent of sin to have a clear conscious.
- Submission. We must be willing to let God be in control.
- Personal Requests. We can share our personal issues with the Lord.
- Faith. We should believe, because of who He is, that everything is taken care of. Thank Him again and agree with His will, using the word Amen (it is done, it is so, so be it).

This may sound like a lot, but your prayer doesn't have to be long and drawn out. You can build your own prayer, or use the Lord's Prayer and go right into your personal petition.

Praying the Scriptures

Praying according to the scriptures is very important. It is key and essential to building your faith in prayer.

For example, sometimes I'm fearful, so I paraphrase a couple of scriptures during prayer about fear. According to scripture, fear causes torment, and that is not of God. One of the affirmations I use is "Perfect love casts out fear, and I receive the perfect love of God in my life. I have no room for fear." The scriptures tell us that God has not given us the spirit of fear but of power, love, and a sound mind, so another affirmation is "I don't receive the spirit of fear in my life because it is not from God, but I have power, I have love, and I have a sound mind."

Praying the scriptures doesn't have to be verbatim. Don't allow the spirit of perfectionism to creep in and overwhelm you because you don't know scriptures by heart.

One idea is to use a notebook or journal, and write down your scriptures and prayers. You can have an intellectual approach to prayer. It doesn't have to be spontaneous or emotional. Your prayer can be intentional and well-thought-out. The Holy Spirit will meet you where you are. When you invite Him into your prayer life, He becomes an instructor, comfort, friend, and guide.

Praying Your Heart

Even though there is a place in prayer for scripted and well-thought-out prayers, there is also a place to pour out the matters of your heart such as joy, pain, and disappointment. My favorite way to handle the unspeakable is to write my prayers. My second favorite is to be like Hannah and pray without sound (1 Samuel 1:12–13); you can pray through tears and sobs, say short prayers, or make simple cries for help.

Expect an Answer

We must be willing to submit to the process of prayer. Prayer is not to be done only out of duty, but we are to pray expecting an answer from God. Beyond that, when we receive the answer, we must respond with obedience. Obedience is the fruit of your faith; it shows God you trust Him. Refusing to walk in faith is to live in rebellion to God's will for your life.

> Ye ask, and receive not, because ye ask amiss, that ye may consume it upon your lusts. (James 4:3)

> But without faith it is impossible to please him: for he that cometh to God must believe that he is, and that he is a rewarder of them that diligently seek him. (Hebrews 11:6)

> Let us hold fast the profession of our faith without wavering (for he is faithful that promised). (Hebrews 10:23)

> Yea, a man may say, Thou hast faith, and I have works: shew me thy faith without thy works, and I will shew thee my faith by my works. (James 2:18)

> But wilt thou know, O vain man, that faith without works is dead? (James 2:20)

For as the body without the spirit is dead, so faith without works is dead also. (James 2:26)

How to Listen for Your Answer

One piece that we seem to miss in prayer is the part where we are to listen. Prayer is two-way conversation. We cast our cares on God, asking Him all our questions and waiting on His answers. We wait for His leading and His guiding. We wait to hear His thoughts. We wait to know His ways. Sometimes, He will speak immediately, but other times, His answer may seem delayed. God responds to us in many ways. His answer can be found in a Bible verse, a song, a reverberating thought, or a still small voice. The key is to be still long enough to hear it.

Once you have received your answer, the next step is obedience. Obedience is better than sacrifice.

And Samuel said, Hath the Lord as great delight in burnt offerings and sacrifices, as in obeying the voice of the Lord? Behold, to obey is better than sacrifice, and to hearken than the fat of rams. (1 Samuel 15:22)

Obedience is better than fasting, praise, and worship. Why seek for His answer if we do not heed His Word? Obedience is sometimes hard, but it is always necessary. You may have to pray for continued guidance and clarity as you walk out your obedience. One of the best ways to show God reverence, honor, and trust is to obey Him. Humble submission is what He desires.

When and Where to Pray

Making Prayer a Priority

As previously mentioned, prayer isn't always the first sought-after solution. As believers, however, prayer should consistently be our priority. We need to consult the Lord early before we begin making decisions.

Daily prayer, whether you pray morning, noon, or night, is unique to your personal life. You must decide to add prayer to your lifestyle. What time will you pray? Will you set aside time every day or once a week? Are you going to prayer to uphold your position (defensive) or to head off the enemy (offensive)?

In Regard to Time

I personally like to spend my quality time in prayer in the morning because mornings are spiritual. My goal is 5 a.m., but sometimes I sleep in until eight; I drink a cup of coffee or tea while I pray, meditate, and study. There is no hard rule for when to pray. My writing coach said she prayed at night, so she'll have her answer before morning and her instructions for the day.

Some people pray during their lunch break or while driving to work. There are also different apps and even prayer watches you can utilize, but we won't get that deep in this book. Do not feel the need to be like someone else. Try out different times, and see what works for you. What allows you to focus and not be rushed?

In Regard to Situations

The best thing to do is seek Him early, before the situation turns to trouble. God can order your steps and help you avoid the pitfalls. Understand that prayer is not a magic solution to everything you don't want to be bothered with. You will still go through trials, but it's all been designed to increase your growth and maturity. Prayer is a tool to keep you in communication with the Father while dealing with the issues of life. It keeps you connected and able to hear clear direction from God.

Where to Pray

You can create a prayer space or use a closet in your home, but you can really pray anywhere. You can pray aloud or in silence. You can journal. We are commissioned to always pray and not faint. We are encouraged to pray without ceasing. When you have consistency in prayer, you don't really need formality to start your conversation with the Father. In your car driving, you can say, "Help with this traffic, Lord," or you may start praising Him during your commute. It doesn't take long for you to feel His presence because you're continuously in communication with Him. The Lord is with you, wherever you go. My pastor teaches us that God is as close to you as your hand is to your elbow.

Pray at the board meeting, baseball game, and doctor's appointment; pray at work, in school, at the council meeting, at the library, and at the restaurant. Pray everywhere.

Types of Prayer

Foundational Prayers

I have found these kinds of prayers to be useful in my spiritual development, especially in hard times, when I don't know what to pray or just need to be closer to God and feel His presence. These prayers can also be starting points when praying for yourself or others. For example, the Lord's Prayer is one of my personal foundation prayers.

Praise and Thanksgiving

This is a prayer expressing admiration and thanks to the Lord for what He has done:

> Praise ye the Lord. Praise God in his sanctuary: praise him in the firmament of his power. Praise him for his mighty acts: praise him according to his excellent greatness. Praise him with the sound of the trumpet: praise him with the psaltery and harp. Praise him with the timbrel and dance: praise him with stringed instruments and organs. Praise him upon the loud cymbals: praise him upon the high

sounding cymbals. Let everything that hath breath praise the Lord. Praise ye the Lord. (Psalm 150)

Repentance

This prayer asks forgiveness of sin, saying that godly sorrow leads to salvation:

> Now I rejoice, not that ye were made sorry, but that ye sorrowed to repentance: for ye were made sorry after a godly manner, that ye might receive damage by us in nothing. For godly sorrow worketh repentance to salvation not to be repented of: but the sorrow of the world worketh death. (2 Corinthians 7:9–10)

Consecration and Sanctification

This is a prayer of dedicating or committing yourself to the service of God. This can include sanctifying yourself, which is setting yourself aside wholly for God's service.

> For I am the Lord your God: ye shall therefore sanctify yourselves, and ye shall be holy; for I am holy: neither shall ye defile yourselves with any manner of creeping thing that creepeth upon the earth. (Leviticus 11:44)

Strength

When you think you can't go any further, simply pray for strength:

> And the Lord said, Simon, Simon, behold, Satan hath desired to have you, that he may sift you as wheat: But I have prayed for thee, that thy faith fail not: and when thou art converted, strengthen thy brethren. And he said unto him, Lord, I am ready to go with thee, both into prison, and to death. (Luke 22:31–33)

Faith

Ask God to strengthen your faith and help your unbelief. You can also declare your faith in prayer. For example, say that you believe He healed the lepers and He can heal you.

> Now faith is the substance of things hoped for, the evidence of things not seen. For by it the elders obtained a good report. Through faith we understand that the worlds were framed by the word of God, so that things which are seen were not made of things which do appear. (Hebrews 11:1–3)

Submission and Surrender

Submission is willingly agreeing and going with the will of God. To surrender is to stop fighting against His will.

> Submit yourselves therefore to God. Resist the devil, and he will flee from you. (James 4:7)

Petition and Supplication

Pray to request God for something desired or needed. This prayer recognizes God as the authority in your life.

> Be careful for nothing; but in every thing by prayer and supplication with thanksgiving let your requests be made known unto God. (Philippians 4:6)

> The Lord hath heard my supplication; the Lord will receive my prayer. (Psalm 6:9)

Wailing and Lamenting

Wailing is a type of cry made from great anguish and grief. Lamenting is having that anguish over events. For example, in the book of Lamentations, it was over cities, places, and so on.

And let them make haste, and take up a wailing for us, that our eyes may run down with tears, and our eyelids gush out with waters. For a voice of wailing is heard out of Zion, How are we spoiled! we are greatly confounded, because we have forsaken the land, because our dwellings have cast us out. Yet hear the word of the Lord, O ye women, and let your ear receive the word of his mouth, and teach your daughters wailing, and every one her neighbour lamentation. (Jeremiah 9:18–20)

Why Is Prayer Your Responsibility?

Prayer is our responsibility because we have been commissioned to pray. As we live obedient lives, we must do as the Word declares. We must pray without ceasing. Just as Jesus spent time alone with the Father, so should we. We need to be consistent communicators with the Father.

Pray without ceasing. (1 Thessalonians 5:17)

Praying always with all prayer and supplication in the Spirit, and watching thereunto with all perseverance and supplication for all saints. (Ephesians 6:18)

Be careful for nothing; but in every thing by prayer and supplication with thanksgiving let your requests be made known unto God. (Philippians 4:6)

I will therefore that men pray everywhere, lifting up holy hands, without wrath and doubting. (1 Timothy 2:8)

Rejoicing in hope; patient in tribulation; continuing instant in prayer. (Romans 12:12)

Continue in prayer, and watch in the same with thanksgiving. (Colossians 4:2)

And he spake a parable unto them to this end, that men ought always to pray, and not to faint. (Luke 18:18)

Watch ye therefore, and pray always, that ye may be accounted worthy to escape all these things that shall come to pass, and to stand before the Son of man. (Luke 21:36)

As previously stated, God does not want to have a one-sided relationship with you. He desires to have a healthy and whole relationship. This relationship is built on love, trust, and communication. Healthy relationships also have reciprocity. Your relationship with God consists of you listening when He speaks and Him listening when you speak. It's having mutual care and concern for one another. My friend Armand says, "Humans are inherently selfish." Being selfish is one thing that we must kill in our flesh. It is our responsibility to pray to strengthen our relationship, to build Godly character in ourselves, and to intercede for others.

8

How to Start

At this point, you should have enough information, inspiration, and encouragement to get started.

1. **Make the Decision.** Decide today that you want to improve your prayer life.

2. **Commit.** Make the commitment to pray at your personally designated time, place, and so on.

3. **Set a Goal.** Whatever your goal is, it must meet the following requirements:

    a. Specific: Well-defined goals should not be vague or broad. For example, "I want to pray more" is too broad. "I want to pray and read my Word every day at 5 a.m." is more specific.

    b. Measurable: Can this be tracked and measured? If we use the previous example, praying every day can be tracked using a calendar or a journal.

c. Achievable: Is this a realistic goal? The above goal, if you work at 5 a.m., would not be realistic.

d. Relevant: Make sure that your goal is related to your part in the prayer conversation. You do not control when, how, or how often God will move according to your prayers, so do not add that to your goal.

e. Time Bound: When do you want this goal to be a part of your life or come to fruition? When will you start the work? When will you want the goal to be established?

4. **Start with Short Prayers.** If you don't already have an idea where you want to start, you can refer to the foundational prayers list in chapter 6.

5. **Build Prayers.** Whether you are using your own prayer list or starting with the foundational prayers, remember to include the fundamentals: thanksgiving, repentance, and submission to God's will.

For example, praying for a job:

Lord, I thank you for this day. I thank you for hearing and answering prayer. Forgive me of my sins, known and unknown. Lord, I'm coming to you because I am in need of a job. I need hours to fit my family life, a livable wage, great benefits, and a retirement plan. Lord, show me the job that you want for me. I submit to your will and your way. In Jesus's name, Amen.

6. **Try Different Styles, Times, and Positions to See What Fits**

A. Different styles of prayer include praying aloud, praying silently, journaling, and singing. You may try them all; whatever you choose is fine.

B. The same is true with the time of day. There are benefits to having a set prayer time. It helps build a relationship. When you pray throughout the day, it is a continued conversation, as opposed to repeating what you prayed earlier.

C. Try different positions: kneeling, standing, walking, lying prostrate (stretched out), sitting.

7. **Just Be Yourself.** God has called us all to pray and never cease or faint. He did not call us to be a carbon copy of anyone else. We all have people we love and admire and inspire us to be better. That's great, but we need to be ourselves in our relationship with the Lord and with our prayer lives. Growth comes with authenticity. Be yourself. God loves you as you are and will help you make any needed changes.

9

Final Thoughts

At this point in the book, I hope that you have been encouraged, uplifted, enlightened, and inspired. I pray that you now have a desire to deepen your communication with the Lord. I pray the Lord will begin to stir your prayer life with urgency and fervor. I pray that you realize how great God's love for you is. I pray you realize that He *wants* you.

Take your time to work through the next section. If you have trouble figuring out what to pray for, especially for spiritual development, work through the prayer prompts and journal. This can also be used as a personal Bible study or devotion.

10

Prayer Prompts and Journaling Pages

Welcome to the prayer prompts and journaling section, where you are provided topics to pray about. On each page, you have space to:

1. **Define the topic.** You can look it up in your favorite secular dictionary or Bible dictionary.

2. **Find scriptures on the topic.** You can use a concordance in the back of your study Bible, a full concordance, or your favorite online search engine. Choose and record the ones that speak to you (feel free to read them in context for better understanding).

3. **Connect the topic to your life**. What do you need to do in your life to line up with the Word you are praying? How do you need the Lord to help you in this area? Remember, there is nothing too big or too small.

4. **Pray.** Prayer time includes being quiet and listening to the Lord. You can pray aloud, pray silently, or write your prayer. Be conscious

of making sure to take time to listen and meditate on the scripture for an answer.

5. **Journal.** Write down your experience. Did you receive your answer right away or later? What was your answer? What feeling did you have before, during, and after prayer?

Repentance

Definition

_____

_____

_____

_____

_____

Scripture(s)

_____

_____

_____

_____

_____

My Connection

_____

_____

_____

_____

Prayer and Journal Space

_____

_____

_____

_____

_____

_____

Faith

Definition

_____
_____
_____
_____
_____

Scripture(s)

_____
_____
_____
_____
_____

My Connection

_____
_____
_____
_____

Prayer and Journal Space

_____
_____
_____
_____
_____
_____
_____

Thanks

Definition

_____

_____

_____

_____

_____

Scripture(s)

_____

_____

_____

_____

_____

My Connection

_____

_____

_____

_____

Prayer and Journal Space

_____

_____

_____

_____

_____

_____

_____

Submission

Definition

_____

_____

_____

_____

_____

Scripture(s)

_____

_____

_____

_____

_____

My Connection

_____

_____

_____

_____

_____

Prayer and Journal Space

_____

_____

_____

_____

_____

_____

_____

Wisdom

Definition

_____
_____
_____
_____
_____

Scripture(s)

_____
_____
_____
_____
_____

My Connection

_____
_____
_____
_____

Prayer and Journal Space

_____
_____
_____
_____
_____
_____
_____
_____

Love

Definition

_____

_____

_____

_____

_____

Scripture(s)

_____

_____

_____

_____

_____

My Connection

_____

_____

_____

_____

Prayer and Journal Space

_____

_____

_____

_____

_____

_____

_____

Protection

Definition

_____

_____

_____

_____

_____

Scripture(s)

_____

_____

_____

_____

_____

My Connection

_____

_____

_____

_____

Prayer and Journal Space

_____

_____

_____

_____

_____

_____

_____

Prayer of Strength

Definition

_____

_____

_____

_____

_____

Scripture(s)

_____

_____

_____

_____

_____

My Connection

_____

_____

_____

_____

Prayer and Journal Space

_____

_____

_____

_____

_____

_____

Prayer of Surrender

Definition

_____
_____
_____
_____
_____

Scripture(s)

_____
_____
_____
_____
_____

My Connection

_____
_____
_____
_____

Prayer and Journal Space

_____
_____
_____
_____
_____
_____
_____

Prayer of Salvation

Definition

_____

_____

_____

_____

_____

Scripture(s)

_____

_____

_____

_____

_____

My Connection

_____

_____

_____

_____

_____

Prayer and Journal Space

_____

_____

_____

_____

_____

_____

_____

Prayer of Deliverance

Definition

_____

_____

_____

_____

_____

Scripture(s)

_____

_____

_____

_____

_____

My Connection

_____

_____

_____

_____

Prayer and Journal Space

_____

_____

_____

_____

_____

_____

_____

Prayer of Commitment

Definition

_____

_____

_____

_____

_____

Scripture(s)

_____

_____

_____

_____

My Connection

_____

_____

_____

_____

Prayer and Journal Space

_____

_____

_____

_____

_____

_____

_____

Prayer of Recommitment

Definition

_____

_____

_____

_____

_____

Scripture(s)

_____

_____

_____

_____

My Connection

_____

_____

_____

_____

Prayer and Journal Space

_____

_____

_____

_____

_____

_____

_____

Prayer for Joy

Definition

_____

_____

_____

_____

_____

Scripture(s)

_____

_____

_____

_____

My Connection

_____

_____

_____

_____

Prayer and Journal Space

_____

_____

_____

_____

_____

_____

_____

Prayer for Peace

Definition

_____

_____

_____

_____

_____

Scripture(s)

_____

_____

_____

_____

_____

My Connection

_____

_____

_____

_____

Prayer and Journal Space

_____

_____

_____

_____

_____

_____

_____

Prayer for Self-Control

Definition

_____
_____
_____
_____
_____

Scripture(s)

_____
_____
_____
_____

My Connection

_____
_____
_____
_____

Prayer and Journal Space

_____
_____
_____
_____
_____
_____
_____

Prayer for Vision

Definition

_____
_____
_____
_____
_____

Scripture(s)

_____
_____
_____
_____
_____

My Connection

_____
_____
_____
_____

Prayer and Journal Space

_____
_____
_____
_____
_____
_____
_____

Prayer for Clarity

Definition

_____
_____
_____
_____
_____

Scripture(s)

_____
_____
_____
_____
_____

My Connection

_____
_____
_____
_____

Prayer and Journal Space

_____
_____
_____
_____
_____
_____
_____

Prayer for Instruction

Definition

_____

_____

_____

_____

_____

Scripture(s)

_____

_____

_____

_____

_____

My Connection

_____

_____

_____

_____

Prayer and Journal Space

_____

_____

_____

_____

_____

_____

_____

_____

LET'S GO DEEPER

The following prayer prompts guide you into specific points of prayer that are part of the broader topics previously covered

I take the specific points of the broader topic to pray specifically and intentionally. It helps broaden the perspective of the main topic.

Submission: Giving Up Your Will

Definition

_____
_____
_____
_____
_____

Scripture(s)

_____
_____
_____
_____

My Connection

_____
_____
_____
_____

Prayer and Journal Space

_____
_____
_____
_____
_____
_____
_____

Submission: Prayer of Consecration

Definition

_____
_____
_____
_____
_____

Scripture(s)

_____
_____
_____
_____
_____

My Connection

_____
_____
_____
_____

Prayer and Journal Space

_____
_____
_____
_____
_____
_____
_____

Submission: Accepting God's Will

Definition

_____

_____

_____

_____

_____

Scripture(s)

_____

_____

_____

_____

_____

My Connection

_____

_____

_____

_____

Prayer and Journal Space

_____

_____

_____

_____

_____

_____

_____

Submission: Submit Your Body to Him

Definition

_____
_____
_____
_____
_____

Scripture(s)

_____
_____
_____
_____
_____

My Connection

_____
_____
_____
_____

Prayer and Journal Space

_____
_____
_____
_____
_____
_____
_____

Submission: Yield Your Members to Righteousness

Definition

_____

_____

_____

_____

_____

Scripture(s)

_____

_____

_____

_____

_____

My Connection

_____

_____

_____

_____

_____

Prayer and Journal Space

_____

_____

_____

_____

_____

_____

_____

Submission: Pray to Release Pride and Arrogance

Definition

_____

_____

_____

_____

_____

Scripture(s)

_____

_____

_____

_____

_____

My Connection

_____

_____

_____

_____

_____

Prayer and Journal Space

_____

_____

_____

_____

_____

_____

Love: Pray about How to Love Yourself

Definition

_____

_____

_____

_____

_____

Scripture(s)

_____

_____

_____

_____

_____

My Connection

_____

_____

_____

_____

Prayer and Journal Space

_____

_____

_____

_____

_____

_____

Love: Pray to Love Your Neighbors, Community, and Leaders

Definition

_____

_____

_____

_____

_____

Scripture(s)

_____

_____

_____

_____

My Connection

_____

_____

_____

_____

Prayer and Journal Space

_____

_____

_____

_____

_____

_____

Love: Pray to Love Your Family, Spouse, and So On

Definition

_____

_____

_____

_____

_____

Scripture(s)

_____

_____

_____

_____

My Connection

_____

_____

_____

_____

Prayer and Journal Space

_____

_____

_____

_____

_____

_____

Love: Pray to Love Your Enemies and the Unlovable

Definition

_____
_____
_____
_____
_____

Scripture(s)

_____
_____
_____
_____
_____

My Connection

_____
_____
_____
_____
_____

Prayer and Journal Space

_____
_____
_____
_____
_____
_____
_____

Love: Pray for God's Love (Agape)

Definition

_____

_____

_____

_____

_____

Scripture(s)

_____

_____

_____

_____

_____

My Connection

_____

_____

_____

_____

_____

Prayer and Journal Space

_____

_____

_____

_____

_____

_____

_____

Love: Pray to Have Brotherly Love (Phileo)

Definition

_____

_____

_____

_____

_____

Scripture(s)

_____

_____

_____

_____

My Connection

_____

_____

_____

_____

Prayer and Journal Space

_____

_____

_____

_____

_____

_____

_____

Love: Pray to Submit Your Romantic Relationships to God (Eros)

Definition

_____

_____

_____

_____

_____

Scripture(s)

_____

_____

_____

_____

_____

My Connection

_____

_____

_____

_____

Prayer and Journal Space

_____

_____

_____

_____

_____

_____

Thanks: Prayer of Praise

Definition

_____
_____
_____
_____
_____

Scripture(s)

_____
_____
_____
_____

My Connection

_____
_____
_____
_____

Prayer and Journal Space

_____
_____
_____
_____
_____
_____
_____

MY FAVORITE RESOURCES

Vine's Complete Expository Dictionary of Old and New Testament Words

*The Strongest: Strong's Exhaustive Concordance
of the Bible, 21ˢᵗ Century Edition*

NIV, KJV, NASB, Amplified, Classic Comparative Parallel Bible

CALL TO ACTION

I want to hear from you. I want to know your testimonies and triumphs. You can reach me at www.RoscheetaMonique.com.

Printed in the United States
by Baker & Taylor Publisher Services